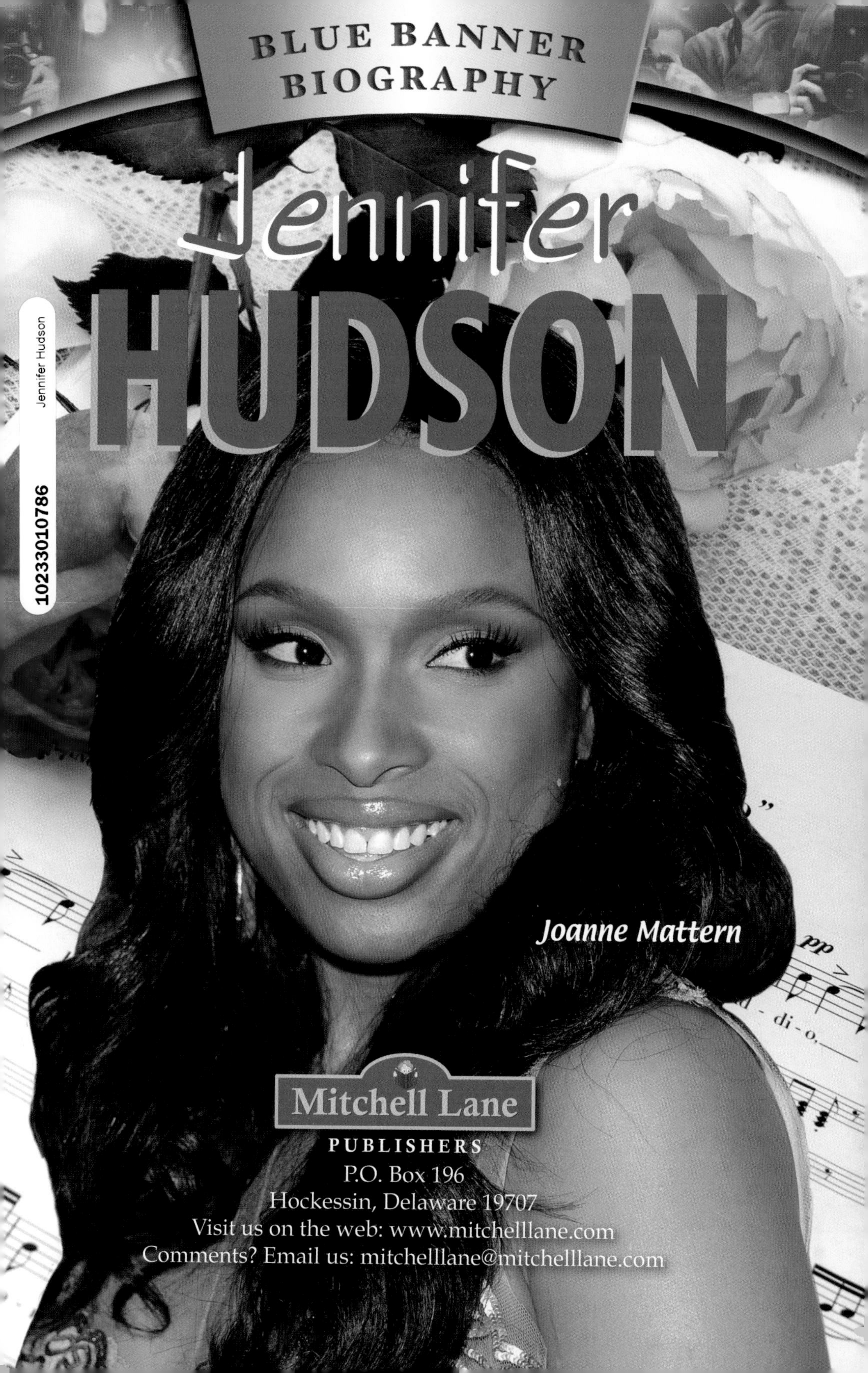

BLUE BANNER
BIOGRAPHY

Jennifer
HUDSON

Joanne Mattern

Mitchell Lane
PUBLISHERS
P.O. Box 196
Hockessin, Delaware 19707
Visit us on the web: www.mitchelllane.com
Comments? Email us: mitchelllane@mitchelllane.com

Mitchell Lane
PUBLISHERS

Printing   1   2   3   4   5   6   7   8   9

Blue Banner Biographies

Adele	Ice Cube	Nancy Pelosi
Alicia Keys	Ja Rule	Natasha Bedingfield
Allen Iverson	Jamie Foxx	One Direction
Ashanti	Jay-Z	Orianthi
Ashlee Simpson	**Jennifer Hudson**	Orlando Bloom
Ashton Kutcher	Jennifer Lopez	P. Diddy
Avril Lavigne	Jessica Simpson	Peyton Manning
Blake Lively	J. K. Rowling	Pink
Bow Wow	Joe Flacco	Prince William
Brett Favre	John Legend	Queen Latifah
Britney Spears	Justin Berfield	Rihanna
Bruno Mars	Justin Timberlake	Robert Downey Jr.
CC Sabathia	Kanye West	Robert Pattinson
Carrie Underwood	Kate Hudson	Ron Howard
Chris Brown	Katy Perry	Sean Kingston
Chris Daughtry	Keith Urban	Selena
Christina Aguilera	Kelly Clarkson	Shakira
Ciara	Kenny Chesney	Shia LaBeouf
Clay Aiken	Ke$ha	Shontelle Layne
Cole Hamels	Kristen Stewart	Soulja Boy Tell 'Em
Condoleezza Rice	Lady Gaga	Stephenie Meyer
Corbin Bleu	Lance Armstrong	Taylor Swift
Daniel Radcliffe	Leona Lewis	T.I.
David Ortiz	Lil Wayne	Timbaland
David Wright	Lindsay Lohan	Tim McGraw
Derek Jeter	Ludacris	Tim Tebow
Drew Brees	Mariah Carey	Toby Keith
Eminem	Mario	Usher
Eve	Mary J. Blige	Vanessa Anne Hudgens
Fergie	Mary-Kate and Ashley Olsen	Will.i.am
Flo Rida	Megan Fox	Zac Efron
Gwen Stefani	Miguel Tejada	

Library of Congress Cataloging-in-Publication Data
Mattern, Joanne, 1963–
Jennifer Hudson / by Joanne Mattern.
    p. cm. — (Blue banner biographies)
Includes bibliographical references and index.
ISBN 978-1-61228-315-9 (library bound)
1. Hudson, Jennifer, 1981– —Juvenile literature. 2. Singers—United States—Biography—Juvenile literature. 3. Motion picture actors and actresses—United States—Biography—Juvenile literature. I. Title.
ML3930.H82M37 2013
782.42164092—dc23
[B]
                                                                                                              2012018303
eBook ISBN: 9781612283869

ABOUT THE AUTHOR: Joanne Mattern is the author of more than 200 nonfiction books for young readers. Her books for Mitchell Lane include biographies of such notables as Michelle Obama, Benny Goodman, Blake Lively, Selena, LeBron James, and Peyton Manning. Mattern grew up listening to big band, jazz, and popular music. She also studied piano and voice for many years. Mattern lives in New York State with her husband, four children, and an assortment of pets.

PUBLISHER'S NOTE: The following story has been thoroughly researched, and to the best of our knowledge represents a true story. While every possible effort has been made to ensure accuracy, the publisher will not assume liability for damages caused by inaccuracies in the data and makes no warranty on the accuracy of the information contained herein. This story has not been authorized or endorsed by Jennifer Hudson.

Blue Banner Biography

Chapter 1
From Dream to Disappointment 5

Chapter 2
Little Girl, Big Voice 8

Chapter 3
Music and Movies 13

Chapter 4
Tragedy and Triumph.................................... 19

Chapter 5
Moving On... 24

Chronology 28

Discography.. 29

Filmography 29

Further Reading 30

Works Consulted... 30

On the Internet.. 31

Index.. 32

When Jennifer Hudson competed on Season 3 of American Idol, her voice captivated audiences. However, she was far from the sleek and sophisticated star she is today.

From Dream to Disappointment

*J*ennifer Hudson had the chance of a lifetime. Just a few months earlier, she had been selected to appear on the reality television show *American Idol.* On the show, singers perform before a panel of three judges, who offer praise and criticism of the singer's performance. Then the television audience votes for the performers they like best. The performer with the lowest number of votes is sent home. Finally, the winner is given a recording contract and the chance to be a huge star. Thousands of singers audition every year to become the next Idol.

Jennifer had dreamed of being a performer ever since she was a child. Being on *American Idol* was a dream come true. Her big voice and colorful personality had won her fans from all over the world. The judges and the famous musicians who mentored the contestants liked Jennifer too. It seemed like nothing could stand between Jennifer and the title of "American Idol."

On April 20, 2004, Jennifer performed "Weekend in New England," a popular Barry Manilow song. Manilow loved her performance, and so did the judges. Judge Randy

Jennifer Hudson had once been rejected as a backup singer for Barry Manilow. However, she made a better impression on the recording star when she performed Manilow's classic song, "Weekend in New England," on American Idol.

Jackson told Jennifer, "That was unbelievable—you just get better and better every week." It seemed like Jennifer would sail into the next round of the competition.

Then the unthinkable happened. Host Ryan Seacrest announced the "bottom three." Those were the three performers who had received the lowest number of votes. One of the bottom three was Jennifer Hudson. Seacrest gave Jennifer and her fans the bad news—she had received the lowest number of votes. It was time for Jennifer to leave *American Idol.*

Jennifer looked stunned and sad as she received the news. The other contestants were shocked. Some even began to cry. Jennifer, however, behaved like a true professional. She sang one last time. Then she left the *American Idol* stage.

Fantasia Barrino, LaToya London, and Jennifer Hudson wait anxiously for host Ryan Seacrest to announce the results on the April 21, 2004, American Idol *show.*

Many people were very upset when Jennifer was voted off *American Idol*. Jennifer, however, was not one of them. She later wrote in her autobiography, "I didn't care if I won or not. As far as I was concerned, my dream had already come true when I was allowed to sing for millions of Americans . . . It was time for me to take another step."

Losing *American Idol* might have ended Jennifer's dreams forever. However, this young lady from Chicago was a survivor. She would go on to bigger and better things after her disappointment on *American Idol*. On that night in 2004, no one could imagine the amazing things Jennifer Hudson would achieve.

Little Girl, Big Voice

*J*ennifer Kate Hudson was born on September 12, 1981, in Chicago, Illinois. Her father, Samuel Simpson, was a bus driver, and her mother was a secretary named Darnell Donnerson. Although Jennifer always calls Samuel Simpson her father, some sources indicate that he may actually be her stepfather. Jennifer had an older brother named Jason and an older sister named Julia.

The Hudson family lived in a Chicago neighborhood called Englewood. Englewood has some of the worst poverty and crime rates in all of Chicago. To Jennifer and her family, however, Englewood was home. The Hudsons lived in a large house with plenty of room for a big family. Jennifer's mother was very involved in her children's lives. She made sure the children studied hard, stayed out of trouble, and felt loved. Jennifer later told reporter Nick Curtis of the *London Evening Standard,* "We were poor but we thought we were rich, because we had everything we needed."

Music was a very big part of Jennifer's life. The radio was always on at home, or records were playing on the stereo, or Jennifer's mother and grandmother were singing. They especially liked gospel music, the type of music they sang in church. The Hudson family was very religious and they attended the Pleasant Gift Missionary Baptist Church several times a week. Jennifer's favorite part of the church services was the music.

It was clear early on that Jennifer had a talent for music. When she was a very young girl, Jennifer was in church during choir practice. The choir was trying to hit a very high note, but none of the members could manage to hit it. Suddenly little Jennifer opened her mouth and hit the note perfectly. Her godmother said, "Mark my words, this child is going to sing."

Jennifer's family supported her singing. Her grandmother, Julia Kate Hudson, often sang to her. She encouraged her granddaughter to

The Hudsons lived in a large house with plenty of room for a big family. Jennifer's mother was very involved in her children's lives.

sing in church, and by the time she was seven years old (pictured left), Jennifer had joined the choir.

As soon as she joined the choir, Jennifer began pestering the director to give her a solo. However, the choir director thought she was too young. Jennifer recalled sitting in the bathroom at home, crying because she was never asked to sing a solo.

Finally, when she was a teenager, Jennifer was given her chance to shine with one solo, followed by another. She continued to sing many solos over the years as her voice grew even more powerful. "I became aware that I could move [people] with my music and I liked the way it felt," Jennifer later wrote.

Not only did Jennifer's family love music, they also loved to eat. And like everyone else in her family, she was big. "Trust me," she wrote in her autobiography, "when it comes to food, the Hudsons don't play around." Large meals were always on the table. Jennifer wrote, "It gave my mama a lot of joy to make meals for her kids. She especially loved making hot breakfasts . . . Before school, we filled our plates with bacon, ham or sausage, pancakes, waffles, eggs, and biscuits . . . Oh, that food was so good." Jennifer did not think much about her weight as she was growing up, but it would become an issue for her as she got older.

> *It was clear early on that Jennifer had a talent for music. When she was a very young girl, Jennifer was in church during choir practice.*

As Jennifer entered her teens, she began singing at weddings, baptisms, and parties all over Chicago. She also competed in talent shows. Jennifer didn't always win, but she gained more confidence every time she performed. On one occasion, she was horrified when a competitor hid the cassette tape with her music on it just before she got up to sing. Not one to be stopped, Jennifer went onstage anyway—and learned to bring a back up in the future!

Jennifer Hudson graduated from Dunbar High School in 1999.

Jennifer suffered several painful losses as a teenager. In 1998, when Jennifer was sixteen, her beloved grandmother died. Just a year later, her father died. Despite her sorrow, Jennifer continued to pursue her dreams.

Jennifer graduated from high school in 1999 and moved to Oklahoma to attend Langston University. Langston has one of the best choral music programs in the nation. Jennifer enjoyed her classes and did well, but she was very homesick. It wasn't long before she returned to Chicago and enrolled in Kennedy-King College.

While she attended school, Jennifer continued to perform. But she soon discovered that many people couldn't see past her size. Jennifer auditioned for singing groups and was rejected because of the way she looked. She later wrote in her autobiography, "I didn't fit the image. I didn't see this at the time . . . I honestly thought that my talent was the thing that should, or should not secure jobs for me. I didn't fully grasp how important image was in show business."

Jennifer's worst experience came when she was nineteen years old and weighed 236 pounds. She auditioned to be a backup singer for singer-songwriter Barry Manilow. Jennifer gave an impressive performance with a gospel song, so she was stunned when she didn't get the job. It wasn't until years later that she realized she had lost out because of her weight. It was a difficult lesson to learn.

In 2003, Jennifer Hudson performed on a Disney cruise ship. Eight years later, on January 19, 2011, she was honored by being named godmother of the new Disney Dream cruise ship.

Music and Movies

*I*n January 2001, Jennifer got a small part in her first professional theater production. A theater in Chicago was putting on a performance of *Big River,* a musical based on Mark Twain's classic novel *The Adventures of Huckleberry Finn.* Doing the show was an important milestone for Jennifer. "That's when I knew I could actually make a living doing this," she told the *Chicago Sun-Times.* Jennifer decided to leave school and become a professional musician.

Jennifer performed in *Big River* for two years. Then, in 2003, she became a performer on a Disney cruise ship. For six months, Jennifer performed in a musical based on the Disney movie *Hercules.* She enjoyed the experience, but performing in fancy costumes aboard a moving, rolling ship could be a challenge!

When Jennifer finished her time with Disney, her friend and manager Walter Williams III gave her some big news. He wanted her to audition for season three of *American Idol.* Jennifer wasn't really interested, but Walter had already bought the plane tickets. So in the summer of 2003, Jennifer and Walter headed to the Georgia Dome in Atlanta to audition.

Jennifer joined thousands of people in the Georgia Dome, all hoping for a place on the show. Jennifer had to go through three auditions. First, she sang in front of a few producers seated at a table on the football field in the Georgia Dome. Jennifer did well and was asked to return to Atlanta a few weeks later. For her second audition, she sang for the show's executive producers. Jennifer was nervous, but she belted out a song called "The Power of Love" by Celine Dion. The producers were impressed. They asked Jennifer to fly out to Pasadena, California, to audition in front of the show's judges.

After making it into the final group of twelve contestants, Jennifer *performed on* American Idol *twice a week.*

In California, Jennifer finally met Randy Jackson, Paula Abdul, and Simon Cowell, the judges who appear on the television show. Jennifer performed a song by soul legend Aretha Franklin. Randy and Paula told Jennifer she was "brilliant" and "the best singer we've heard so far." Simon Cowell spoke the words every contestant wanted to hear: "See you in Hollywood!" Jennifer was officially in the running to be the American Idol!

After making it into the final group of twelve contestants, Jennifer performed on the show twice a week. Every week had a different theme, such as Motown or songs from the 1980s. Jennifer also had the opportunity to work with music legends who came in to mentor and help the performers. One mentor was Elton John, who became one of Jennifer's biggest supporters.

Other people were not as impressed with Jennifer. Although everyone knew she had a powerful voice, Jennifer once again faced criticism for her weight. In her autobiography, Jennifer recalled one of the music directors complaining that everything about her was "too big." Jennifer was annoyed and responded, "Isn't that what being a star is? Stars are larger than life!" She refused to let other people's prejudices get in her way.

Jennifer did well on *American Idol* for a while. But on April 21, 2004, she became the sixth contestant to be voted off the show. However, that was not the end of Jennifer's time with *American Idol*. The top ten finalists on the show

Jennifer and Elton John became friends after he mentored her on American Idol. *Six years later, in 2010, they attended the 18th Annual Elton John AIDS Foundation Academy Awards Party in West Hollywood, California.*

went on tour during the summer. Jennifer loved the tour and enjoyed sharing the stage with her fellow performers. She later wrote, "Once the tension of the competition had gone away, it was just pure fun." Jennifer remained friends with several of her fellow contestants and says there will always be a strong bond between them.

After her success with Dreamgirls, it wasn't long before Jennifer was back on the charts again.

In 2005, Jennifer was given an amazing opportunity. She was asked to audition for a movie called *Dreamgirls.* This movie was based on a hit Broadway musical about three female singers who become stars during the 1960s. Jennifer auditioned for the part of Effie White, the lead singer of the group, who is later pushed out of the spotlight because of her weight. It was a story Jennifer had experienced in her own life. "I knew exactly how it felt to be judged for your looks," she wrote in her autobiography. "I knew what it was like to not get jobs because you didn't fit an 'image.' I knew what it was like to deal with people who thought there were things more important than talent. This was a role I had to play."

Jennifer got the part. When *Dreamgirls* was released in 2006, she became a sensation for her role as Effie. One of the highlights of the movie came when Jennifer sang "And I Am Telling You I'm Not Going." The song expresses her pain and outrage at being forced out of the life she loved.

Jennifer's performance was so powerful that she was nominated for an Academy Award for Best Supporting

Jennifer's movie debut in Dreamgirls *made her an award-winning actress. Here she poses with her Golden Globe Award for Best Supporting Actress on January 15, 2007. Just a few weeks later, she would win an Academy Award.*

Actress. And much to her surprise, she won. Jennifer became one of only a few actors to win an Oscar for her first movie. Jennifer also received many other awards, including a Golden Globe, an NAACP Image Award, and a Screen Actors Guild Award. Her recording of "And I Am Telling You I'm Not Going" also became a top 20 hit on the *Billboard* R&B/Hip-Hop chart.

After her success with *Dreamgirls,* it wasn't long before Jennifer was back on the charts again. In September 2008, she released her first album, *Jennifer Hudson.* The album

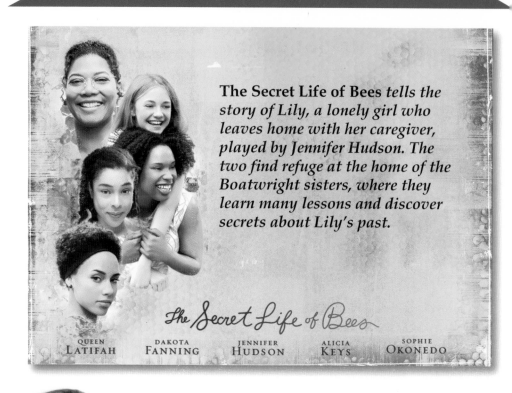

The Secret Life of Bees *tells the story of Lily, a lonely girl who leaves home with her caregiver, played by Jennifer Hudson. The two find refuge at the home of the Boatwright sisters, where they learn many lessons and discover secrets about Lily's past.*

The Secret Life of Bees

QUEEN
LATIFAH

DAKOTA
FANNING

JENNIFER
HUDSON

ALICIA
KEYS

SOPHIE
OKONEDO

debuted at Number Two on the *Billboard 200* chart. The first single, "Spotlight," went to Number One on *Billboard's* R&B/Hip-Hop Chart. Jennifer's album was named the Best R&B Album at the Grammy Awards a few months later.

In 2008, Jennifer appeared in two more movies: *Sex and the City,* and *The Secret Life of Bees.* In August that same year, Jennifer sang "The Star-Spangled Banner" at the Democratic National Convention in Denver.

The year 2008 had been an amazing one for Jennifer Hudson. Unfortunately, the year would end in tragedy.

Tragedy and Triumph

On October 24, 2008, Jennifer Hudson was on top of the world. She had recently fallen in love with a man named David Otunga and the two had gotten engaged on her birthday that September. Jennifer had planned to visit her family in Chicago that weekend in October, but David, who was a professional wrestler, was appearing at a show in Florida. He asked Jennifer to go with him and she agreed. That decision may have saved her life.

On that Friday, Jennifer received terrible news. Her sister Julia had come home to discover their mother and brother had been murdered in their home in Chicago. Julia's son, seven-year-old Julian King, was missing. Everyone hoped for Julian's safe recovery, but his body was found in a car a few days later. Julia had recently separated from her husband, William Balfour, who was arrested for the murders. In May 2012, Balfour was found guilty of all three murders.

For a few months after the murders, Jennifer hid from the world. She stayed with family and close friends but did not appear in public. "It was like I was outside of myself,"

Jennifer poses with her sister, Julia, her mother, Darnell, and her nephew, Julian. Jennifer's world was rocked by tragedy when Darnell, Julian, and Jennifer's brother, Jason, were murdered in 2008.

Jennifer later said in VH1's *Behind the Music.* "I [had] to get adjusted to who I am now." Jennifer also relied on prayer to help her through those difficult days. "I would pray when I get up in the morning and pray before I lay down at night," she told VH1.

Just over three months after the tragedy, Jennifer made her first public appearance. On February 1, 2009, she sang "The Star-Spangled Banner" at the Super Bowl, which was televised all over the world. The performance was very moving and even some of the football players standing on the field had tears in their eyes as Jennifer sang.

Jennifer Hudson returned to the stage with a moving performance of the national anthem at Super Bowl XLIII.

Jennifer was back in public in a big way. Just a week after her Super Bowl performance, she sang at the Grammy Awards. Jennifer also received a Grammy for her debut album. She was thrilled when one of her idols, Whitney Houston, presented the award. Houston called Jennifer "one of the greatest voices of our time."

Jennifer also became involved in charity work. Because of what had happened to her family, she wanted to assist other families who were also dealing with the loss of loved ones. In October 2008, Jennifer and her family announced the creation of the Hudson-King Foundation for Families of Slain Victims. The foundation provides food, clothing, and grief counseling to families who have lost relatives to violent crimes.

Jennifer also received a Grammy for her debut album. She was thrilled when one of her idols, Whitney Houston, presented the award.

Jennifer performed many times throughout 2009 and 2010. She sang "Will You Be There" at Michael Jackson's memorial service in July 2009, and in 2010, she contributed her voice to the single "We Are the World: 25 for Haiti." All the profits from this song were given to survivors of the earthquake that struck Haiti in 2010.

But Jennifer had an even bigger reason to rejoice in 2009. On August 10, her son David Daniel Otunga, Jr. was born. Jennifer was thrilled to be a mother. She told VH1 that she wants to give her son "the same love and the same upbringing as my mother gave us, and I know for sure that way he'll be loved."

Having a baby changed Jennifer's life. For years, her weight had gone up and down. Jennifer had never cared what other people thought about the way she looked. But having David made her realize that she needed to change her life. "Becoming a mother brought on tremendous responsibilities," she wrote, "but none greater than the obligation I felt to get healthy to be there for my son."

Determined to keep the memory of her nephew alive, Jennifer established the Julian D. King Gift Foundation. She appeared with her son, David, and her sister, Julia, at a Foundation celebration in Chicago.

Jennifer changed how she was eating. Instead of junk food and big meals, she ate smaller portions of vegetables, fruits, and lean meats and fish. She also began exercising several times a week. The biggest breakthrough, however, came when she talked to someone from a weight-loss program called Weight Watchers. Jennifer joined the program and within a year, she had lost eighty pounds. Jennifer became a spokesperson for Weight Watchers and inspired many people with her story.

Moving On

Jennifer spent the summer of 2010 in South Africa filming the title role of a movie called *Winnie.* The movie tells the story of the South African political activist Winnie Mandela. Unfortunately, the movie received poor reviews and was not a success.

As soon as Jennifer finished filming *Winnie,* she began recording her second album. *I Remember Me* was released on March 22, 2011. She wanted the album to be "more personal than the first album, and just more me." R&B singer Ne-Yo, who worked with Jennifer, told E! Online, "She's gone through a lot over the last year, so she has a lot to talk about. She's definitely gotten stronger." *I Remember Me* quickly reached Number Two on the *Billboard* 200 chart, selling 165,000 copies in the first week. The album's first single, "Where You At" rose to Number Ten on the *Billboard* R&B/Hip-Hop chart.

Jennifer also continued as a spokesperson for Weight Watchers. She appeared in television commercials and talked to reporters about her new healthy lifestyle. Jennifer was especially proud of the fact that seventy-five members

Jennifer's weight loss motivated her to help others. She teamed up with Weight Watchers for its annual Lose for Good campaign to fight hunger and obesity. During the campaign, Weight Watchers pledged a donation of up to one million dollars to charity depending on how much weight its members lost.

of her family had lost a total of more than 2,000 pounds on the program. She is excited to be an inspiration to family members, friends, and even strangers who admire her weight loss. She wrote in her autobiography, "Part of my drive to keep at it myself is so I can continue to set a positive example for my family and others."

Jennifer's rising popularity also gave her new status as a fashion star. She told *Good Housekeeping* magazine that she loves getting dressed in the morning because "I feel like a doll that I get to dress up! It's crazy. They have to drag me off the red carpet!" However, Jennifer says in her autobiography that even though she's lost a lot of weight, she is still the same girl. "I don't want to go and put everything out there on display."

In 2012, Jennifer published her autobiography. *I Got This: How I Changed My Ways and Lost What Weighed Me Down* told the story of her life and career. The book also went into detail about her weight loss and the lessons she's learned along the way. Perhaps the book's most important message is about taking charge of your life. "We all have the power to choose how we are going to handle every situation

Family remains the most important thing in Jennifer Hudson's life. She and David Otunga are the proud parents of David, Jr., whose birth motivated Jennifer to change her life.

Singer, actress, and author, Jennifer Hudson signed copies of her best-selling autobiography, I Got This: How I Changed My Ways and Lost What Weighed Me Down, *in Los Angeles, California, in January 2012.*

we are faced with throughout our lives," Jennifer wrote. These are words she tries to live by every day.

Jennifer continues to perform and appear on television. One of her most inspiring performances was at the Grammy Awards on February 12, 2012. Whitney Houston had passed away unexpectedly the day before. As part of a tribute to Houston during the awards ceremony, Jennifer sang a beautiful version of "I Will Always Love You," one of Houston's most powerful and well-known songs.

Throughout her life, Jennifer has known both pain and triumph. Back in 2004, when she left *American Idol,* she told the audience, "It's been a struggle, it hasn't been easy, but if it's not worth working hard for, it's not worth it at all. So I'm proud of the struggle that I've been going through, and I'm making it. I'm a survivor."

1981 Jennifer Kate Hudson is born on September 12.

1988 Begins singing in the church choir.

1999 Graduates from high school and attends Langston University, then Kennedy-King College.

2001 Appears in a Chicago theater production of *Big River*.

2003 Performs on a Disney cruise ship; auditions for *American Idol*.

2004 Appears on *American Idol* and finishes in seventh place; performs on the American Idol's LIVE! U.S. tour.

2006 Appears in the movie *Dreamgirls*.

2007 Wins the Academy Award for Best Supporting Actress for *Dreamgirls*.

2008 Releases the album *Jennifer Hudson*; appears in the movies *Sex and the City* and *The Secret Life of Bees*; becomes engaged to David Otunga; Jennifer's mother, brother, and nephew are murdered.

2009 Performs "The Star-Spangled Banner" at Super Bowl XLIII; wins a Grammy Award for Best R&B Album; she gives birth to her son David Daniel Otunga, Jr.

2010 Performs on the "We Are the World: 25 for Haiti" charity single; loses eighty pounds on Weight Watchers and later becomes a spokesperson for the program.

2011 Appears in the title role of the movie *Winnie*; releases her second album, *I Remember Me*.

2012 Publishes her autobiography, *I Got This*; performs a tribute to Whitney Houston at the Grammy Awards.

2011   *I Remember Me*

2008   *Jennifer Hudson*

2006   *Dreamgirls: Music from the Motion Picture*

2004   *American Idol, Season 3: Greatest Soul Classics*

2012   *The Three Stooges*

2011   *Winnie*

2009   *Fragments*

2008   *Sex and the City*
         The Secret Life of Bees

2006   *Dreamgirls*

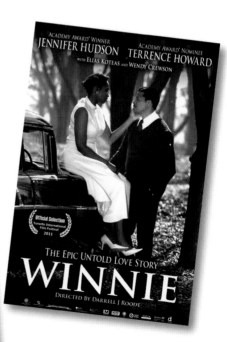

FURTHER READING

Books

Cartlidge, Cherese. *Jennifer Hudson.* Farmington Hills, Michigan: Lucent Books, 2011.

Nagle, Jeanne M. *Jennifer Hudson.* New York: Rosen Publishing Group, 2008.

Snyder, Gail. *Jennifer Hudson.* Broomall, Pennsylvania: Mason Crest, 2009.

West, Betsy. *Jennifer Hudson: American Dream Girl.* New York: Price Stern Sloan, 2007.

Works Consulted

Curtis, Nick. "Oscar Hope Hudson Brings Down the House." *London Evening Standard,* January 25, 2007. http://www.thisislondon.co.uk/film/article-23383042-oscar-hope-hudson-brings-down-the-house.do

Dunn, Jancee. "Winning (and Losing) Big." *Good Housekeeping,* February 2012.

Elder, Robert K. "Though Hudson's Career Took Off, Her Family Here Kept Her Grounded." *Chicago Tribune,* October 26, 2008. http://articles.chicagotribune.com/2008-10-26/news/0810250298_1_jennifer-hudson-hip-hop-albums-mother

"The Final Act: Jennifer Hudson." *20/20.* ABC, March 18, 2011. Television.

Hoekstra, Dave. "Living the Dream: Jennifer Hudson Brings Truth, Clarity to 'Dreamgirls' Role." *Chicago Sun-Times,* December 17, 2006.

Hudson, Jennifer. *I Got This: How I Changed My Ways and Lost What Weighed Me Down.* New York: Dutton, 2012.

"Jennifer Hudson." *Behind the Music.* VH1, June 28, 2010. Television.

Malkin, Marc. "Who Wants a Whitney and Jennifer Hudson Duet?" E! Online, September 18, 2009. http://www.eonline.com/news/marc_malkin/who_wants_whitney_jennifer_hudson_duet/145009

Mascia, Kristen. "Inside Jennifer Hudson's Amazing Weight Loss." *People*, January 16, 2012.

Perry, Beth. "Jennifer Hudson Announces Foundation for Murder Victim Families." *People*, October 30, 2008. http://www.people.com/people/article/0,,20236848,00.html

"Season 3, Episode 30." *American Idol.* Fox Broadcasting Company, April 21, 2004. Television.

On the Internet

Jennifer Hudson: AmericanIdol.com http://www.americanidol.com/archive/contestants/season3/jennifer_hudson

Jennifer Hudson Biography: *People* http://www.people.com/people/jennifer_hudson/biography

Jennifer Hudson: IMDb http://www.imdb.com/name/nm1617685/bio

Jennifer Hudson Official Site http://www.jenniferhudson.com/us/home

Weight Watchers http://www.weightwatchers.com/util/art/index_art.aspx?tabnum=1&art_id=84581

INDEX

Abdul, Paula 14
Academy Award 16–17
American Idol 4–7, 13–16, 27
"And I Am Telling You I'm Not
    Going" 16, 17
Balfour, William 19
Barrino, Fantasia 7
Big River 13
Billboard 17, 18, 24
Cowell, Simon 14
Dion, Celine 14
Disney 13
Donnerson, Darnell 8–10,
    19–20
Dreamgirls 16–17
Dunbar High School 11
Englewood 8
Franklin, Aretha 14
Golden Globe Awards 17
Grammy Awards 18, 21–22, 27
Hercules 13
Houston, Whitney 21–22, 27
Hudson, Jason 8, 19
Hudson, Jennifer Kate
    birth 8
    early career 10–13
    education 11, 13
    family 8–11, 19–26
    murder of family 19–21
    sings with church choir
        9–11
    weight 10, 11, 15, 16, 22–23,
        24–26
Hudson, Julia 8, 19–20,23
Hudson, Julia Kate 9, 11

Hudson-King Foundation 22
I Got This 26–27
I Remember Me 24
Jackson, Michael 22
Jackson, Randy 5–6, 14
Jennifer Hudson (album) 17–18
John, Elton 15
Julian D. King Gift Foundation
    23
Kennedy-King College 11
King, Julian 19–20
Langston University 11
London, LaToya 7
Manilow, Barry 5–6, 11
Ne-Yo 24
Otunga, David 19, 26
Otunga, David Daniel, Jr. 22–
    23, 26
Pleasant Gift Missionary Baptist
    Church 9
Seacrest, Ryan 6–7
Secret Life of Bees, The 18
Sex and the City 18
"Spotlight" 18
"Star-Spangled Banner, The"
    18, 21
Super Bowl 21
VH1 21, 22
"We Are the World: 25 for
    Haiti" 22
"Weekend in New England"
    5–6
Weight Watchers 23–25
Williams, Walter III 13–14
Winnie 24